Understanding the Apostolic Sphere

Apostle Dr. Perry Jackson

Understanding the Apostolic Sphere

By: Apostle Dr. Perry Jackson

Published by J. Elaine Writes
www.jelainewrites.com

No part of this book may be reproduced, stored in a retrieval system, or transmitted in any form or by any means electronic, mechanical, photocopy, recording, or any other- except for brief quotations in printed reviews, without the prior written consent of the author and/or publisher.
Scriptures taken from the King James Version of the Holy Bible. Scriptures marked NASB are from the New American Standard Bible. All rights reserved.

Edited by: J. Elaine
Cover Design by: Design X MEV

This document is published by J.Elaine Writes located in the United States of America. It is protected by the United States Copyright Act, all applicable state laws and international copyright laws.

Copyright © 2019 by Apostle Dr. Perry Jackson

Printed in the United States of America
ISBN: 978-1-7332352-0-4 (Trade paper)

Dedication

I dedicate this book to the men and women who have continued to support me with their prayers.

To my family members, who in spite of all odds, stood fast with me through this journey. This book would not be happening had it not been for your support and love. This book has been a long time coming. In the midst of the challenges I faced on this journey, thank God I had your support, along with faith in God, which also gave me the strength to make this journey.

I would also like to thank all those who would not let me give up when times would get hard and it looked like there was no place to turn nor go. They encouraged my faith in the Lord. Again, I say thank you.

I would like to give a special dedication to my wife, Apostle Dr. Denise V. Jackson, for her love and drive. You have been my greatest supporter. Thank you so much for helping me to make this book finally come to life. Thank you and I love you.

Table of Contents

Dedication .... I.

Introduction 1

Moving in the Apostolic 5

The Apostolic Commission 10

On the Cutting Edge 15

Understanding the Apostolic/"First Things First" 25

It's Time For An Upgrade 33

Behind the Veil 37

Introduction

The purpose of this book is to help bring clarity to the men and women who sense the call of God in this honor of being selected and consecrated of Jesus as an Apostle and/or one of the Fivefold ministry gifts and walk in what may seem to be unfamiliar territory. For some, there has been a pull on your heart to go into this area of ministry, but there are some reservations due to fear of not being sure that you are equipped to carry out the assignment and/or meet the oppositions that is to come. You may also find it difficult because of the challenges that come with the call. So, as you become more engaged in your walk and more knowledgeable about this office(s) you sense God is calling you into, you will come to understand the grace that comes with such office(s) is sufficient for you.

In 2 Corinthians Paul describes a purpose for God's Grace**,** *"For this thing I besought the Lord thrice that it might depart from me. And he said unto me, my grace is sufficient for thee; for my strength is made perfect in weakness."* I know that this scripture may refer to the Apostle Paul having a thorn in his flesh, but I believed that it is just as vital here as it reflects God's Grace being sufficient. As you read this book, my desire is that it would help you on your journey as an Apostle of The Lord Jesus and as an Officer in the Kingdom of God. This is not a tell all book because there are now so many books that are out that can give you much more, but I pray that you will glean some revelation from this one and that it will cause you to not be afraid to accept the assignment that God has placed upon you. When I accepted this assignment, there was not much information out there for me and for others like myself to go and get any understanding from. There were those whom God knew could handle the opposition that they would face coming from **behind the veil** and walking in this journey- exploring this new territory. These men and women of God stood head and shoulders above so many, and with faith in what they believed God had given to them, they feared not the enemy and his demonic attacks; and should they had feared, they stood firm on the Word of God and this new revelation that God was bringing to life before them. You must understand that this was not a new revelation really, but a revived one that was being released in a kairos moment. Kairos is an ancient Greek word meaning the right or opportune moment (the supreme moment). These generals established the groundwork for this dispensation of time and continue to build upon the foundations which the early apostles had laid so that individuals like me and others who would come behind them would have some guidelines set for us to follow. Each generation is a brick in this structure. The blood, sweat, and tears, along with prayer and fasting, is the mortar between the bricks placed on top of the foundation that was laid by the Lord Jesus Christ and His Disciples; and now that continues through us who have come behind them. *Eph. 2:10 For we are his workmanship, created in Christ Jesus unto good works, which God hath before ordained that we should walk in them.* **So, I decree that fear will not overtake you as you press forward into your assignment. You will find yourself moving forward into new territories, lands, regions, and areas that have not been explored in this level of your ministry.** For some, it may seem like everything is well and going good, but as time will tell through prayer, warfare, travailing, and the seeking of God's plan, you will find that it is not church as usual and things will not be the same nor will things be as they seem in time past, present, and future. As you read this book**, I decree that you receive a clearer understanding of the grace that you have been called to and that your walk becomes more secure in who has called you and what *measure of rule* that you are to walk therein.** The Apostle Paul says, "***I therefore, the prisoner of the Lord,*** *beseech ye that you walk worthy of the vocation wherewith ye were called, with all lowliness and meekness, with longsuffering, forbearing one another in love; endeavoring to keep the unity of the Spirit in the bond of peace."*

Remember, you did not make a mistake when you were commissioned by God to walk this calling out, because God does not make mistakes. Everything that you have experienced, has been preparing you for that which is to come; so, do not feel as if you are not qualified to do what you have been called to do, but remember "everything that you need is already inside of you." *Jeremiah 1:5 says, "Before I formed thee in the belly I knew thee; and before thou camest forth out the womb I sanctified thee, and I ordained thee a prophet unto the nations."*

Moving in the Apostolic
Acts 2:42-44

Acts 2:42 *"And they continued steadfastly in the apostles' doctrine and fellowship, and in breaking of bread, and in prayer. And fear came upon every soul: and many wonders and signs were done by the apostles. And all that believed were together, and had all things common."* **(King James Version)**

ACTS 2:42 They were continually devoting themselves to the apostles' teaching and to fellowship, to the breaking of bread and to prayer. (NASB)

ACTS 2:43 Everyone kept feeling a sense of awe; and many wonders and signs were taking place through the apostles. (NASB)

AC 2:44 And all those who had believed were together and had all things in common." (NASB)

If I am going to follow the teaching of the apostles, then I need to know what it is that they were teaching. What was this doctrine or teaching that Acts 2:42 is referring to? If I am to move in the Apostolic, then I need to know more about their teaching so I can understand what is expected of me. How am I going to see what they saw and do what they did except I follow the model that is placed before me. If I am going to see miracles, signs, and wonders manifest, then I need know in my heart by faith and through revelation what Jesus did. Jesus left us an example through the model of the early church what is to be expected of us to follow.

In the Book of Hebrews, the sixth chapter, Paul makes mention of the doctrine of Christ by saying, ***"Therefore leaving the principles of the doctrine of Christ, let us go on unto perfection; not laying again the foundation of repentance from dead works, and of faith toward God, of the doctrine of baptisms, and of laying on of hands, and of resurrection of the dead, and of eternal judgement.*** So, since this is the teaching of Christ, the apostles continued in this teaching as they taught the church. And as they followed Christ they also saw the move of God take place in their lives and in the lives of those that followed them. Paul says "follow me as I follow Christ," so if you are going to move in the apostolic, then you are going to need to follow the example that is before you. Jesus did not just talk of miracles, but he demonstrated them on His journey throughout His travels. Now with the understanding that this doctrine is the foundation that needs to be laid, the Apostle Paul goes on to say in ***Hebrews 6:3,***

"And this will we do, if God permit." So, what is this that we are to do? That would be what Paul said in Hebrews 6:1, *"Let us go on unto perfection."* One of the purposes of an Apostle along with the other Apostolic Gifts and Graces is to bring the people of God on one accord in the revelation knowledge of the Lord Jesus Christ so that they will operate under an Apostolic Grace and carry out the Apostolic Commission given in Matthew 28:19, 20; *[19] Go ye therefore, and teach all nations, baptizing them in the name of the Father, and of the Son, and of the Holy Ghost: [20] Teaching them to observe all things whatsoever I have commanded you: and, lo, I am with you always, even unto the end of the world. Amen.*
Which we will discuss in the next chapter more in detail.

Ephesians 3 profoundly states that the mysteries of heaven are revealed to both the apostles and the prophets. *Ephesians 3:5 says, "Which in other ages was not made known unto the sons of men, as it is now revealed unto his holy apostles and prophets by the Spirit;"* As the Lord shares His knowledge and wisdom with you, there is no standing still. *Ephesians 4:11-16, [11]And he gave some, apostles; and some, prophets; and some, evangelists; and some, pastors and teachers;*

¹²For the perfecting of the saints, for the work of the ministry, for the edifying of the body of Christ:

¹³Till we all come in the unity of the faith, and of the knowledge of the Son of God, unto a perfect man, unto the measure of the stature of the fullness of Christ:

¹⁴That we henceforth be no more children, tossed to and fro, and carried about with every wind of doctrine, by the sleight of men, and cunning craftiness, whereby they lie in wait to deceive;

¹⁵But speaking the truth in love, may grow up into him in all things, which is the head, even Christ:

¹⁶From whom the whole body fitly joined together and compacted by that which every joint supplieth, according to the effectual working in the measure of every part, maketh increase of the body unto the edifying of itself in love.

Apostle Paul states that "And He gave some, apostles, and some prophets...... *'For the perfecting of the saints'*, (for the maturing of the saints), *'for the work of the ministry'*, (to carry out the assignment that you are given), *'for the edifying of the body of Christ'"*, (to build up the believer). One of things that God said that brought me into a strong conviction that the Apostolic Grace is in full stands, is that next verse. In verse 11 he says, *"Till we all come in the unity of faith, and of the knowledge of the Son of God, unto the measure of the statue of the fullness of Christ."* When you look at the church now, you will see that we have not come to the unity of faith.

When you begin to receive the revelation of the mysteries of heaven that is being poured into you, your mind can now understand that thing God is revealing to you concerning Him. It is[1] at that point your mind and Jesus' mind becomes one in the spirit, so when Philippian 2:5 says, *"let this mind be in you which is also in Christ Jesus."* What we must understand is that because God is a progressive God and that he is always moving forward and because you are created in His image and after His likeness, you are as He is. Which means that per Genesis 2, when God breathed into you His breathe, He blew Himself into you and all that He is, you are and with that you are in a forward momentum. So, as you begin to understand who you are in Christ and the abilities that you have, you then begin to do what Jesus did, when He said, the works that I do, you will also be able to do and greater works than these.

The Apostolic Commission
Matthew 28:19-20

The Apostolic Commission in Matthew 28:19-20 states;

MT 28:19 **" *Go therefore and make disciples of all the nations, baptizing them in the name of the Father and the Son and the Holy Spirit,***
MT 28:20 ***teaching them to observe all that I commanded you; and lo, I am with you always, even to the end of the age.* "**

The word *commission* means; the authority granted to a person or organization to act as an agent for another, also it is a job or task given to a person or a group, especially an order to produce a product or piece of work or a charge and a direction. To commission someone is to authorize them. Now the Greek-English Lexicon gives a broad definition for the word apostle as one who is sent on a mission, a commissioned representative of a congregation, a messenger for God, a person who has the special task of founding and establishing churches. The term apostle is derived from the Greek word apostolos meaning "one who is sent away or to send on a mission and/or assignment. In other words, you have a mandate or an order to carry out the assignment that you have been given. This released the disciples into the world to minister unto it by calling forth those and establishing the kingdom of God in the earth realm. We must understand that this command is not just a command to go into the world and preach or teach the gospel, but it comes with the authority of the one who gave it, so when we carry out this command, we do so walking in the power and authority of the one who sent us. Because this is an apostolic commission, understand that there is a grace that also comes with the assignment. *Ephesians 4:7- But to each one of us grace has been given as Christ apportioned it."* To move in the apostolic, you must understand that there is an anointing that comes with each dispensation that you are walking in. What you will be doing on this assignment will take more than just your natural ability to face the opposition you will encounter. You will not be able to walk worthy of the vocation without knowing that you have power that is given you to perform the task that you are assigned to. Remember *Ephesians 6:12* says, *"For we wrestle not against flesh and blood, but against principalities, against powers, against the rulers of the darkness of this world, against spiritual wickedness in*

high places. " The Apostle Paul states that we are ambassadors of the Lord Jesus Christ.

An **ambassador** is an official envoy; a diplomatic agent of the highest rank accredited to a foreign government or sovereign as the resident representative of his own government or sovereign or appointed for a special and often temporary diplomatic assignment**.** In other words, we have been given the authority of Christ Jesus to carry out His great command and assignment. The Apostolic Commission that is given to the church requires us to invade new territories and regions. Even though we have been given the land and/or territories; we must understand that this new territory once belonged to others who possessed it which could be and/or is also considered hostile territory due to the types of strong-hold(s) that is determined through the surveying of that territory. Jesus says in the Great Commission "to go and make disciples in all the nations…and teach them to obey everything that I have commanded you." We must understand that there are those who have been in these nations teaching what the world and Satan would want them to know. And that these teachings and learnings have been going on for some territories for centuries and for others, even longer. The power of darkness that has ruled these regions for centuries will not be willing to give them up without a fight. We must understand that these strongholds have been in these areas for quite some time and will not give this territory up without a fight. These strongholds are made up of demonic influences that have been building over time. There are different types of strongholds in each region that have established the mind-sets of the people of that territory.

So, to carry out this order of the commission, we must recognize the authority that is in us. ***Eph. 6:10 says, "Finally, my brethren, be strong in the Lord and in the power of his might."*** We are to understand that everything we are to do; we are to do it in the power of Christ. For it is in his power and by his strength that we can and are able to fulfill our assignment and any challenges that we will face. As stated before, to fulfill this great commission, we are going to need power. Acts 1:8 says *AC 1:8* ***"but you will receive power when the Holy Spirit has come upon you; and you shall be My witnesses both in Jerusalem, and in all Judea and Samaria, and even to the remotest part of the earth."***

We are given this authority and power to accomplish the assignment that is given unto us by God. This power/grace is not for personal gain or self exhortation, but for the witness of Christ Jesus in the world.

We are given specific instructions on how we are to do this. He says first in Jerusalem, Judea, Samaria and then into the utter-most parts of the earth.

On the Cutting Edge
Joshua 3:2-6

"Jos 3:2 After three days the officers went throughout the camp,
Jos 3:3 giving orders to the people: "When you see the ark of the covenant of the LORD your God, and the priests, who are Levites, carrying it, you are to move out from your positions and follow it.
Jos 3:4 Then you will know which way to go, since you have never been this way before. But keep a distance of about a thousand yards between you and the ark; do not go near it."
Jos 3:5 Joshua told the people, "Consecrate yourselves, for tomorrow the LORD will do amazing things among you."
Jos 3:6 Joshua said to the priests, "Take up the ark of the covenant and pass on ahead of the people." So they took it up and went ahead of them."

To be on the cutting edge means walking in an apostolic grace that causes you to have a pioneering anointing. To **pioneer** is to open or prepare for others to follow; (2) to originate or take part in the development of. Apostle John Eckhardt put it this way in his book called *Proton* that:

"pioneers lead the way, open up, found, forge, break new ground, initiate, establish and prepare. So as cutting edge believers and apostolic people, you are pioneers and as pioneers you are pathfinders and as pathfinders you are trailblazers and as trailblazers you will be explorers and as explorers you are forerunners and if forerunners you will be innovators. To pioneer means to set in motion, to start the ball rolling, to take the first step, to take the initiative, to break new ground, to break the ice, to take the lead, to lead the way, blaze the trail, to institute, to inaugurate, a founder, to establish, to set up, to lay the first stone, to introduce, to launch, to usher and to lay the foundation."

It is this apostolic anointing that pushes us forward to move into new territories and into new frontiers to obtain the goals of fulfilling our commission. There must be something or someone who is influencing and/or causing you to move into the direction that is not the norm. So, we need to have a spirit that is a cutting-edge spirit. When we look at the Holy Spirit, it is he that sees us where we are even at the beginning of the offset of our journey. In Acts 1:8; he tells us that we will have the ability, authority and power to go into areas that we are to be sent.

Ac 1:8 ***But you will receive power when the Holy Spirit comes on you; and you will be my witnesses in Jerusalem, and in all Judea and Samaria, and to the ends of the earth."***

Many of these new regions are un-chartered and have not come into the place that God is bringing the church into and so this is where some of the hostility comes from. A good example of being sent into a new place is found in the book of Acts *"Ac 19:1* ***While Apollos was at Corinth, Paul took the road through the interior and arrived at Ephesus. There he found some disciples***
Ac 19:2 ***and asked them, "Did you receive the Holy Spirit when you believed?"***
They answered, "No, we have not even heard that there is a Holy Spirit."
Ac 19:3 ***So Paul asked, "Then what baptism did you receive?"***
"John's baptism," they replied.
Ac 19:4 ***Paul said, "John's baptism was a baptism of repentance. He told the people to believe in the one coming after him, that is, in Jesus."***
Ac 19:5 ***On hearing this, they were baptized into the name of the Lord Jesus.***

Ac 19:6 **When Paul placed his hands on them, the Holy Spirit came on them, and they spoke in tongues and prophesied.**

Ac 19:7 **There were about twelve men in all."**

The Apostle Paul is faced with bringing present truth unto those that were still walking in past knowledge As the Chief Apostle of New Works International Fellowship of Churches; it is our mission to bring the people of God out of the wilderness into the promises of God, out of tradition into the fullness of God and to become all that God has called them into. And so, God equips His church with power and gives us the authority to go into these areas to do the work that he has assigned to us. He will not send you into a place to perform a task without making sure that you can fulfill the assignments that have been placed in your hand. It is God's responsibility to supply you with the tools and equipment to perform your assignment, but it's your responsibility to carry out the assignment with the tools and equipment given to you. Remember that there is a grace that is upon you that grants you the ability to fulfill your task. There is no excuse that can be given or that we can state that will allow for us not to fulfill our duties and responsibilities. There is a grace that is set upon you to help you accomplish your assignment (Ephesians 4:7).

The New American Standard says; *Eph. 4:7* *"But to each one of us grace was given according to the measure of Christ's gift."*

The Amplified Bible put it this way; *Eph 4:7* *"Yet grace (God's unmerited favor) was given to each of us individually [not indiscriminately, but in different ways] in proportion to the measure of Christ's [rich and bounteous] gift."* If you do not accomplish your assignment, it is only because you have aborted it and not because God did not give unto you everything that you will need to complete your assignment. Apostle Paul said that He (God) will supply your every need according to his riches in glory in Christ Jesus our Lord.

According to Jeremiah, everything that you need is already in you to allow you to perform your assignment. Jeremiah says in the Amplified Bible,

Jer. 1:5 *"Before I formed you in the womb I knew [and] approved of you [as My chosen instrument], and before you were born I separated and set you apart, consecrating you; [and] I appointed you as a prophet to the nations."*

So, it is our responsibility along with the help of the Holy

Spirit to develop that which is in us so that we may prefect our vocation wherein we have been called.

Now you must also realize that because you are on the cutting edge and moving into these new unchartered territories, it also means that your tents and borders will be enlarging. These boundaries are invincible lines or borders between what is and what is not. In the book of Joshua, God tells Joshua that every place that your feet shall walk upon, that have I given unto you. Anytime God enlarges your tent, your responsibilities become greater and with greater responsibility comes greater accountability. You cannot expect God to give you more and not expect more from you. "To whom much is given, much is required." We will be discussing this later in another chapter.

In this chapter, there are several points I want to show you about being on the cutting edge that will strengthen you to success.

First, you are an ambassador and as an ambassador you walk in the authority of the one by which you represent. You are carrying out His commands, His instructions and His directives; and because you are carrying out His commands, you do it with His backing and support. In other words, you have all of heaven at your command to call upon (Ephesians 1:3).*Eph. 1:3* ***"Give praise to the God***

and Father of our Lord Jesus Christ. He has blessed us with every spiritual blessing. Those blessings come from the heavenly world. They belong to us because we belong to Christ."

Second, cutting edge people do not live on excuses; because of what God has given unto us, we are without excuse. Everything that we need is available to us and to understand this, we need to seek him for directions on how to apply the correct set of rules and tools to the proper job. One of our biggest reasons for not being able to succeed is that we use the wrong rules on an assignment that calls for another set of rules. You can not use baseball rules in a basketball game. Some of the terminology may be the same and even sound alike, but the meaning of them are different and so to apply a self-same rule that is different in this assignment will cause more harm than success. Romans 8:26-27 tells us that the Spirit of God will help us in our weakness.

Ro 8:26 *"In the same way, the Spirit helps us in our weakness. We do not know what we ought to pray for, but the Spirit himself intercedes for us with groans that words cannot express.*

Ro 8:27 ***And he who searches our hearts knows the mind of the Spirit, because the Spirit intercedes for the saints in accordance with God's will."***

Per Ephesians 4:11-15, *Eph. 4:11* ***"It was he who gave some to be apostles, some to be prophets, some to be evangelists, and some to be pastors and teachers,***

Eph 4:12 ***to prepare God's people for works of service, so that the body of Christ may be built up***

Eph 4:13 ***until we all reach unity in the faith and in the knowledge of the Son of God and become mature, attaining to the whole measure of the fullness of Christ.***

Eph 4:14 ***Then we will no longer be infants, tossed back and forth by the waves, and blown here and there by every wind of teaching and by the cunning and craftiness of men in their deceitful scheming.***

Eph 4:15 ***Instead, speaking the truth in love, we will in all things grow up into him who is the Head, that is, Christ. God have made provision to make sure that we as apostolic believers understand how to use every advance that is available."***

Third, your actions always speak louder than your words. James said faith without works is dead. To be on the cutting edge means that there is work involved. What you do demonstrates who you are in Christ greater than what you say; so your actions speak greater than your words.

Forth, your ability to handle a $2.99 crisis will determine your ability to handle a million dollar one. Jesus said that if you are faithful over little then he will make you ruler over much. We must be able to manage small things and assignments before we can be trusted to handle greater responsibilities. You would not give your three-year-old child your keys to your brand new car and tell him to take it. He must, through time, earn your confidence over the years, prove himself responsible by showing you that he can handle small assignments, and then after that, you will now feel that you can trust him with a greater task. So, God does to us as we do also to our children.

Fifth, cutting edge leaders walk by faith and not by sight. This is not as easy as some would have you to believe because it means moving only by the leading of the Holy Spirit. Your senses are not in control. Your five senses (touch, taste, smell, sound, and sight) do not direct your ability to move forward into unfamiliar territory, it is your sixth sense (trust) that motivates you and that kind of trust is your belief in the Word of God by which you are walking in and on. In Matthew 14:26-31, Jesus is walking on the sea and the disciples see him walking toward them and Jesus said unto them "Be of good cheer; it is I; be not afraid," and when Peter saw and recognized him, he said to Jesus if it be you, allow me to come unto you and Jesus said to him; Come and Peter stepped out of the ship and began to walk on water." What Peter was stepping out on was the word that Jesus spoke. In the beginning, Peter stepped out on faith and his faith had substance and that substance was the word that Jesus spoke. It was not until he began to follow his five senses that he began to sink. As cutting edge believers, we walk by faith and not by sight.

Understanding the Apostolic/ "First Things First"
1 Corinthians 12:28

1Co 12:28 "And in the church God has appointed first of all apostles, second prophets, third teachers, then workers of miracles, also those having gifts of healing, those able to help others, those with gifts of administration, and those speaking in different kinds of tongues."

As we begin to walk in first things first, we will also begin to realize and recognize that as apostolic ministries, standards are set and it is expected that we come up to the place that God has established for his people. The churches have been going through a purifying process. The reason that the church is going through these experiences are because of the spirit shifting in the body of Christ. This shift is not in levels, as we keep hearing, but the dimension of the level that you are in. It is not that He's not elevating from level to level, but those whom he has or will elevate are developing and are becoming mature in the fullness of that level. God wants His people to be well rounded, to walk in the spirit of excellence and be mature believers that can handle whatever is coming. God gave me a prophetic word some years ago when He spoke and said "the flood gates are going to open and when the gate opens the people of God will not be able to handle it. Everyone will not be able to deal with the magnitude of this outpouring." In 1997, God began to speak to me concerning those who have been behind the veil and that He has been preparing those who are behind the veil for such a time as this. In 2000, He spoke and said that the veil had been cracked open just enough to allow those on the outside to see a portion of His glory and to see that which he had been preparing behind the veil. And now we are going to see more of His glory through the shifting that is about to take place in the body of Christ. The church is crying out to the Lord for this dispensation to come forth. In Isaiah 43:18-19 God tells Israel to "remember not the former things, and not dwell on the past. See, I am doing a new thing, now it shall spring up, do you not perceive it, I am making a way in the desert, and streams in the wasteland."

There is a more excellent way. God has been saying we must raise our standards and to do that, we must ***excel*** in our gifts and callings. Apostle Paul states in 1 Corinthians 14:12, "Even so ye, for as much as ye are zealous of spiritual gifts, seek that ye may excel to the edifying of the church." Now the root word for **excellence** is **excel** and we must be excellent in everything we do for the Lord.

As apostolic people, we are to set order and set the order per Titus 1:5-11; ***Tit 1:5 The reason I left you in Crete was that you might straighten out what was left unfinished and appoint elders in every town, as I directed you.***

Tit 1:6 An elder must be blameless, the husband of but one wife, a man whose children believe and are not open to the charge of being wild and disobedient.

Tit 1:7 Since an overseer is entrusted with God's work, he must be blameless—not overbearing, not quick-tempered, not given to drunkenness, not violent, not pursuing dishonest gain.

Tit 1:8 Rather he must be hospitable, one who loves what is good, who is self-controlled, upright, holy and disciplined.

Tit 1:9 He must hold firmly to the trustworthy message as it has been taught, so that he can encourage others by sound doctrine and refute those who oppose it.

Tit 1:10 For there are many rebellious people, mere talkers and deceivers, especially those of the circumcision group.

Tit 1:11 They must be silenced, because they are ruining whole households by teaching things they ought not to teach—and that for the sake of dishonest gain."

The Apostle Paul gives Titus some sound teaching on how to present himself as an apostolic leader as well as what to look for in the body. Because there is such a high standard in place before us, we are expected to show ourselves approved unto God, which is our reasonable service. When God separated Israel from the other nations unto Himself, He set standards before them which caused them to become a model unto the rest of the world.

As a people of vision, we understand that God is a visionary and as such, He is also a strategist, and because He is both a visionary and strategist and we are made in His image and after His likeness, we have the same DNA as God our Father. God is beginning to release the prepared ones from behind the veil into their destiny. These apostolic people have been given specific administrative and operational strategies that will perfect the body of Christ so they can bring Ephesians 4 closer to perfection. These are trained experts in their vocation to come and teach, train and develop the people of God so they can walk worthy of the vocation wherein they are called.

There are eight basic areas that require strengthening in the church. These are the areas by which the devil will not be able to penetrate and bring division into the body of Christ.

First: *Prayer.* Intercession and Fervent prayer must become a vital part of worship. How are we going to take the kingdom in the natural, if we have not subdued it in the spirit realm first? The Bible says that "the kingdom suffers violence and the violent take it by force.

Second: *Praise and Worship.* The praise and worship teams must know in whom they are glorifying so their ushering in the people of God is not a task, but a joy.

Third: *Evangelism.* Evangelism and outreach go hand-n-hand. The life of the church is winning the lost to God. The purpose of what we do to bring glory to God is by telling everyone who He is.

Forth: *Prophetic Ministry.* Prophets and prophetic teams move the church forward. If there is no prophetic ministry in the church, then it will become stagnant and without growth.

Fifth: *Deliverance.* Deliverance also moves the church forward and causes it to progress because it drives out evil spirits and opens the way for the people to possess the land.

Sixth: *Teaching.* Teachers and their teams need to move in knowledge, understanding and in revelation. It is where clarity come and with clarity, life and not death. Hosea says, *Hos 4:6* *"my people are destroyed from lack of knowledge."*

Seven: *Mission.* This is a part of the apostolic mandate and Apostolic Commission for the church.

Eight: *Pastoral and Cell Leaders.* Pastors and pastoral teams are an important part of watching over and maintaining the spiritual growth of the saints. Within the apostolic ministries, there needs to be a place where the body would be on one accord that no matter where you are in the church or denomination you are in, it would be on one accord. It is essential that the body of Christ be on one accord as it relates to Jesus' death, burial, and resurrection. Acts 2:42-47 speaks about following the apostle's doctrine and what took place when the church is on one accord. God will add to the church when we come together.

Ac 2:42 ***They devoted themselves to the apostles' teaching and to the fellowship, to the breaking of bread and to prayer.***

Ac 2:43 ***Everyone was filled with awe, and many wonders and miraculous signs were done by the apostles.***

Ac 2:44 ***All the believers were together and had everything in common.***

Ac 2:45 ***Selling their possessions and goods, they gave to anyone as he had need.***

Ac 2:46 ***Every day they continued to meet together in the temple courts. They broke bread in their homes and ate together with glad and sincere hearts,***

Ac 2:47 *praising God and enjoying the favor of all the people. And the Lord added to their number daily those who were being saved.*

One of Satan's purposes is to divide the church. He knows that when we become as one, nothing is impossible to them that believe. When we look back in the Old Testament at the building of the Tower of Babel, it states that the world had one language and all things in common. They began to build a tower that would go up into heaven and when God saw this *Ge 11:6* **The LORD said, "If as one people speaking the same language they have begun to do this, then nothing they plan to do will be impossible for them."** Now, if the people who were not saved and didn't even have the Holy Spirit, could accomplish this, how much more could those of us who are in Christ Jesus and do have the Holy Spirit perform if we were to come together on one accord. Therefore, Satan wants to keep the church divided, because the moment we come together in Christ Jesus, the devil knows what kind of destruction would be against him and his kingdom.

The apostolic church is set up to restore and embrace the love that God established from the very beginning. God's Love and the Holy Spirit is its driving force. It is essential that the apostolic ministry has a driving force. There must be something powerful enough to motivate and push it forward to conquer all obstacles and challenges that are ahead of us. Therefore, the Love of God and Holy Spirit is what motivates the church to go into these territories and complete its destiny.

It's Time For An Upgrade
Acts 19:1-7

"Ac 19:1 While Apollos was at Corinth, Paul took the road through the interior and arrived at Ephesus. There he found some disciples

Ac 19:2 and asked them, "Did you receive the Holy Spirit when you believed?"

They answered, "No, we have not even heard that there is a Holy Spirit."

Ac 19:3 So Paul asked, "Then what baptism did you receive?"

"John's baptism," they replied.

Ac 19:4 Paul said, "John's baptism was a baptism of repentance. He told the people to believe in the one coming after him, that is, in Jesus."

Ac 19:5 On hearing this, they were baptized into the name of the Lord Jesus.

Ac 19:6 When Paul placed his hands on them, the Holy Spirit came on them, and they spoke in tongues and prophesied.

Ac 19:7 There were about twelve men in all."

Where there has been no knowledge or where there has been a lack thereof, this shift or paradigm shift, will bring revelation and in these revelations, there shall come an up-grade, due to the knowledge that is being released and/or given to those who are open to adhere to the revelation that is given. In Acts 19:1-7, we can see here what happens when knowledge comes. When we talk about this kind of up-grade, we are then talking about having an impartation which is taking what is on the inside of you or someone and imparting it into another. The apostolic anointing can elevate the body of believers from where they are to another level in the spirit. Some time ago the Lord spoke to me and said that "he was going to take what was in him and impart it into me and I was to take that and impart it into others." In other words, it was as if he was saying "all that is in him he would put into me and I am to take all that is in me and put it into others." It is going to take the governmental anointing of the five-fold gifts to bring about such an upgrade. Many believers are walking beneath their ability and privileges due to where they are and by what they have been taught. The time has come and is passing when Jesus says, "the day you hear my voice, harden not your heart". God is a God of progression, He is always moving forward and because He is always moving forward and we are made in His image and after His likeness, we also are to be progressive and moving forward.

This was and is not always the case because the people of God do not want to grow, but because the leaders could only teach what they themselves knew. They either did not know or couldn't understand due to the place that they were in, because of their spiritual growth. We must understand that this does not mean that they were not and are not saved or anointed, but that there is a limit to their revelation and understanding.

We must realize that we are to walk in the spirit of excellence which mandates for us to excel in our gifts. To do the work that God has ordained for us to do, we can not stay in the same frame of mind as were our fore-parents. The Word of God does not change, but the understanding of it causes us to see both God and the fulfillment of The Great Commission becoming a reality. 1 Corinthians 14:12 states that we are to *"seek that ye may excel to the edifying of the church."* Remember that the root word of **excellence** is the word **excel**. God does not want us to just be average, but to excel in every area of our lives.

Ephesians 4:1 said in the Amplified Bible;

Eph 4:1 *"I THEREFORE, the prisoner for the Lord, appeal to and beg you to walk (lead a life) worthy of the [divine] calling to which you have been called [with behavior that is a credit to the summons to God's service,"*

Upgrade is a process per Mark 4:26-29 that said,

"*Mk 4:26* **And He said, The kingdom of God is like a man who scatters seed upon the ground,**

Mk 4:27 **And then continues sleeping and rising night and day while the seed sprouts and grows and increases—he knows not how.**

Mk 4:28 **The earth produces [acting] by itself—first the blade, then the ear, then the full grain in the ear.**

Mk 4:29 **But when the grain is ripe and permits, immediately he sends forth [the reapers] and puts in the sickle, because the harvest stands ready."**

Behind the Veil

In 1998, God began to speak to me concerning a shift that was going to happen in the church and the Body of Christ. The Lord has been keeping behind the veil those who he was preparing for the next change of leaders and the next dispensational move in the upcoming season. This is to be a changing of the guards and there were those who you would least expect to be in that gathering. Those whom from the view of man would seem to be unlikely to be selected to lead the next move of God along with people who would help usher in this new wave. While everyone is looking to the left and to the right, what God was going to do was bring them from behind the veil. Those he was working on to be able to go into the religious arena and bring about a shift in the church, from church thinking to kingdom thinking and bring it with a more strategic plan on invading the kingdom of Satan by simply using the Word of God as their stance. They must be able to stand even when no one else would stand with them. Ezek. 2:3-7 puts it this way; *Ezek. 2:3* ***And He said to me, I send you, son of man, to the children of Israel, to a rebellious nation that have rebelled against Me. They and their fathers have transgressed against Me even to this very day.***

Ezek. 2:4 ***And the children are impudent and hard of heart. I send you to them and you shall say to them, Thus says the Lord God.***

Ezek. 2:5 ***And they, whether they will hear or refuse to hear—for they are a rebellious house—yet shall they know and realize that there has been a prophet among them.***

Ezek. 2:6 ***And you, son of man, be not afraid of them, neither be afraid of their words; though briers and thorns are all around you and you dwell and sit among scorpions, be not afraid of their words nor be dismayed at their looks, for they are a rebellious house.***

Ezek. 2:7 ***And you shall speak My words to them whether they will hear or refuse to hear, for they are most rebellious.***

There are those who he has had behind the veil, who were being prepared for what he is about to do in this next transition. They were going through preparation and everything that they had experienced has only been getting them ready for the next move of God in the earth realm. All the hurts, pains, stresses, disappointments, struggles, and put downs; physical, mental and emotional issues that they have had to endure are only setting them up for what God has in his mind for them. For the most part, we could not understand why we were going through so much and others seem to be experiencing the blessing of the Lord. Being behind the veil will not be an easy thing to handle, but the Lord said that "I have you covered and you are not in this alone." Being behind the veil and going through this type of training and not knowing why you are experiencing the things that you are experiencing, may place you in a state of confusion and dismay. It makes you feel as though you have missed God in what you are doing. For myself, I kept asking the same questions and had not yet known for sure the answer or if I was even asking the right questions to get the right answer. God kept speaking to me about those that were behind the veil and so for years I would go to different churches and ministries and declare what the Lord had told me concerning them who have been hidden from everyone's view; as if I was sounding an alarm to those who may have been in those places to be ready, for their time would soon come to be released at the proper time into their destiny. As the years moved forward, around 2005 God began to show me that he had begun to crack open the curtain so that those on the outside would be exposed to those that were behind the veil and for those who were back there to look out, but those on the outside could look in and get a glimpse of them and the glory of God upon those who he has been preparing.

This shift in the atmosphere is not accepted by everyone, especially by those who do not see and/or understand what God is doing in these last days as he is preparing the church for his second coming. Just as there are those who help the bride to get everything ready and adorned for the walk down the aisle, so are those who God has now put into place to help the church make ready for the groom as she prepares to meet him in the air.

As we read the Word of God, one would have to seek God concerning His meaning of His writing, because as you read areas of it, there are gaps in between parts of some of the incidents that takes place and if you do not ask Him to fill in the gaps, you can misunderstand the essence of the content. I bring this up because no one brought to my attention this as I was growing up in the Lord. This is where He gives revelation and clarity to the Five-fold ministry gift to understand those things which seem to be confounding to the world and to those who refuse to hear what the Spirit should say to the church.

As I stated when I began this book, its purpose is to help bring some clarity to those who sense the call on their life walk in an arena that is specifically assigned to them by God. Know this, when you except who you are in this, know that no matter what happens in life, God got you covered through it all. Though you might fill alone on this journey, you are not, for God is with you, "even unto the end of the world."

www.ingramcontent.com/pod-product-compliance
Lightning Source LLC
Chambersburg PA
CBHW032105040426
42449CB00007B/1186